THE TROILUS–CRESSIDA STORY FROM

CHAUCER TO SHAKESPEARE

by

Hyder E. Rollins.

PMLA Vol. 32   pp. 383-429
September, 1917

XVI.—THE TROILUS–CRESSIDA STORY FROM CHAUCER TO SHAKESPEARE

Viewed from any angle Shakespeare's *Troilus and Cressida* is an unattractive play. The heroine is a wanton. Ulysses reads her at a glance and finds

> language in her eye, her cheek, her lip,
> Nay, her foot speaks; her wanton spirits look out
> At every joint and motive of her body.[1]

He sets her down at once as "a daughter of the game," and at every opportunity the foul-mouthed Thersites corroborates this description. " They say Diomedes keeps a Trojan drab," he monologizes, "and uses the traitor Calchas his tent. I'll after; "[2] and in the rather awkward scene in which Cressida's perfidy is revealed to Troilus, he gleefully whispers: "Any man may sing her, if he can take her cliff. She's noted."[3] Even in this scene, however, Shakespeare is not devoid of sympathy; Cressida's qualms of conscience as she pins on Diomedes the sleeve Troilus had given her, as she feels herself yielding, are touching. Yet Cressida is a woman of loose morals, and Troilus himself, though irreproachable as a warrior, in his relations with her hardly warrants one's sympathy. There is no mistaking the sensuality of his desires when for the first time he is to meet her alone:

> I am giddy; expectation whirls me round.
> The imaginary relish is so sweet
> That it enchants my sense: what will it be,
> When that the watery palates taste indeed,
> Love's thrice repured nectar?[4]

---

[1] IV, v, 54 ff.
[2] v, i, 104.
[3] v, ii, 10.
[4] III, ii, 19 ff.

1

Cressida, too, knows what to expect from the visit. Pandarus describes her as blushing and fetching her "wind so short, as if she were afraid with a sprite;" [5] but it is to be feared that her agitation arose less from modesty and timidity than from a sense of elation at having at last caught a lover of exalted rank. She is not at all shocked by her uncle's disgustingly coarse jests nor by his efforts to hurry the assignation. Of course Elizabethan audiences were not repelled by such scenes, and Shakespeare himself saw no particular moral significance in them, as is proved by the plots of *All's Well* and *Measure for Measure;* nevertheless, there is no other scene in all his plays so frankly sensuous as this. Nothing can be more different than his treatment and Chaucer's of the morning after the lovers' meeting. In Chaucer one thinks of the ardent devotion of the lovers; in *Troilus and Cressida* the details are so coarsened that one thinks only of the animal nature of their love. In the play Pandarus has been joking boisterously with Cressida (an incident borrowed from Chaucer, although in the poem Troilus is not present during this scene), when a knock is heard at the door. After the conversation that then takes place (IV, ii, 36-40), Troilus may protest as much as he wishes about the purity of his love for Cressida, but we cannot help feeling that his animal nature is most deeply stirred by her loss.

Since its surreptitious publication in 1609 and its admission, apparently as an afterthought, into the First Folio, *Troilus and Cressida* has always been a puzzle. It seems hardly necessary to enumerate the widely divergent theories that have been advanced to explain Shakespeare's purpose in writing the play. The two most striking theories, that the play was Shakespeare's contribution to the

[5] III, ii, 32.

war of the theatres and that it was a deliberate vulgariza-
tion of the Greek and Trojan heroes and of Cressida
caused by Shakespeare's jealousy of the rival poet, Chapman, are not now generally believed. But a peculiar view
is still held by almost all critics. A Chaucerian scholar's
comment will serve as well as any: Shakespeare has ap-
proached the love story " in a spirit of bitter cynicism and
blackest pessimism. The love story . . . is merely disgusting . . . To crown all, the final worthlessness of
Cressida, and the breaking heart of Troilus, are inter-
preted to us by the syphilitic mind of Thersites, whose
whole function in the play is to defile with the foulness of
his own imagination all that humanity holds high and
sacred. . . . It remains one of the puzzles of criticism that
such a work should ever have proceeded from the great
soul of Shakespeare." [6]

Is this true? Did Shakespeare himself debase the
story? Does he pursue Cressida, as other critics have said,
with relentless hatred? Dr. Small briefly hinted at the
reason for the loose character of Shakespeare's Cressida,[7]
but Professor Tatlock, almost alone among editors and
commentators, has, I think, correctly analyzed the play.
He writes: " Shakespeare came to the material of this play,
then, precisely as he came to that of the English historical
plays, finding incidents and characters largely fixed before-
hand, and too intractable to be greatly modified, even had
he wished to modify them. It is as a historical play, in
the Elizabethan sense, that it should be regarded; often
serious, sometimes verging on the tragic, but pervaded
with comedy." [8]

---

[6] R. K. Root, *The Poetry of Chaucer*, pp. 104-105.
[7] *The Stage Quarrel*, p. 155.
[8] *Troilus and Cressida*, Tudor edition, pp. xix-xx. In articles on
" The Siege of Troy in Elizabethan Literature, Especially in Shake-

This *is* almost the whole secret of the play, and my own
remarks may, in the main, seem to be only a reinforcement
of Professor Tatlock's conclusions. The history of Troilus
and Cressida and Pandarus from Chaucer to Shakespeare
has not before been traced, however, although this is almost
essential for a genuine understanding of what Shakespeare
tried to do, of what indeed he did do, and it reveals also
facts of some importance in regard to Henryson and
Chaucer. When Sir Sidney Lee writes in 1916: "At one
point the dramatist diverges from his authorities with
notable originality. Cressida figures in the play as a heart-
less coquette; the poets who had previously treated her
story . . . had imagined her as a tender-hearted, if frail,
beauty, with claims on their pity rather than on their
scorn. But Shakespeare's *innovation* is dramatically effec-
tive, and deprives fickleness in love of any false glam-
our ";[9] or when an editor of Miss Porter's experience can
write as late as 1910, " Shakespeare evolves his own name
[Cressida]. He seems to use Caxton's form as a whole,
prefaced by Chaucer's initial letter,"[10] surely it is time to
consider the history of the love story and the lovers.

speare and Heywood " (*Publications of the Modern Language Asso-
ciation of America*, vol. XXX, pp. 673-770) and " The Chief Problem
in Shakespeare " (*Sewanee Review*, April, 1916), which appeared
after the present article was completed, Professor Tatlock has even
more clearly and convincingly developed this view, and has also
called attention to the relation of Heywood's *Iron Age* to Shakespeare's play.

[9] *A Life of William Shakespeare* (1916), p. 370.

[10] *Troilus and Cressida*, First Folio edition, p. 131. It may be
remarked that the two title-pages to the First Quarto run " The
Historie of Troylus and *Cresseida* " and " The Famous Historie of
Troylus and *Cresseid*," the spelling used in the Edinburgh, 1593,
edition of Henryson's *Testament of Cresseid*. Shakespeare's favorite fórm, if indeed he had a favorite, was Cressid, and this had been
used for years before he wrote. Even in MSS. of Chaucer's own
poems the name is found with the spelling " Crisseyde," " Creseyde,"

It was quite in a spirit of prophecy that Chaucer's Criseyde lamented:

> Allas! for now is clene a-go
> My name of trouthe in love, for ever-mo!
> For I have falsed oon, the gentileste
> That ever was, and oon the worthieste!
>
> Allas, of me, un-to the worldes ende,
> Shal neither been y-writen nor y-songe,
> No good word, for thise bokes wol me shende,
> O, rolled shal I been on many a tonge!
> Through-out the world my belle shal be ronge.[11]

Some thirty years after she had thus bewailed her fate, Lydgate, translating Guido at the command of Prince Hal, had to retell her story. He did so with some diffidence, referring his readers to his master Chaucer for a complete and accurate account. Lydgate added nothing to the story, but he was in thorough sympathy with his Cryseyde, bitterly reproved Guido for his slanders of women in general, and tried to excuse Cryseyde in particular because Nature had made her variable.[12] She also escaped harsh words from the author of the Laud *Troy Book* (about 1400), who indeed may have known her only through Guido, and who usually calls her Bryxeida or Brixaida. But when the author tells us that Diomedes struck down Troylus and sent his horse to "Cresseide, ðat fair woman, That sumtyme was Troyle lemman," [13] he perhaps had Chaucer's Criseyde in mind.

"Criseida," "Creseide." In this article the spelling used by the authors who are quoted is retained.

[11] Bk. v, st. 151-152.

[12] In H. Bergen's edition of the *Troy Book* (E. E. T. S., 1906-1910) the story may be followed in Bk. II, ll. 4676-4762, Bk. III, ll. 3664-3754, 4077-4263, 4343-4448, 4619-4659, 4820-67, Bk. IV, 2132-77, 2401-2779.

[13] L. 9053 (ed. Wülfing, E. E. T. S., 1902-03). The main events of the story occur at ll. 9065-92, 13427-38, 13543-64, 14857 ff.

Nor does Caxton's *Recuyell* (1474) concern us, save that in his history of Troylus and Breseyda he, like Lydgate, referred all readers, Shakespeare presumably among them, to Chaucer for further details. Calchas, he writes, "had a passing fayr doughter and wyse named breseyda/ Chaucer in his booke that he made of Troylus named her creseyda "; [14] and again, " Ther was neuer seen so moche sorowe made betwene two louers at their departyng/ who that lyste to here of alle theyr loue/ late hym rede the booke of troyllus that chawcer made/ wherin he shall fynde the storye hooll/ whiche were to longe to wryte here." [15]

During the sixteenth century the story seems to have been constantly on men's tongues, though few people could comprehend the spirit of high comedy and irony in which Chaucer had written. Of the characters as he portrayed them, Pandarus was by far the most dramatic, but naturally enough Pandarus quickly developed into a low comedy figure. On Twelfth Night, 1515/6, at Eltham, Cornish and the Children of the Chapel Royal acted the *Story of Troylous and Pandor.* Cornish himself, " clad in mantle and bishop's surcoat, took the role of Calchas. The children acted the roles of Troilus, Cressid, Diomed, Pandor, Ulysses, and others not named . . . Chaucer's ' Criseyda in widowes habite blak ' remained in the account of the furnishings as ' Kryssyd imparylled lyke a wedow of onour, in blake sarsenet and other abelements for seche mater.' " [16] Pandar, the go-between, had probably, even

---

[14] Ed. H. O. Sommer, vol. II, p. 601.

[15] *Ibid.,* p. 604. These allusions are not in Miss Spurgeon's *Five Hundred Years of Chaucer Criticism and Allusion.* Unless her book is directly referred to, it may be assumed that other allusions to Chaucer noted in this article are not there printed.

[16] C. W. Wallace, *Evolution of the English Drama up to Shakespeare,* Berlin, 1912, p. 48.

in this early play, degenerated into a clown. There was no other way in which to treat him. Not long afterward, Nicholas Grimald, according to Bale, wrote a Latin comedy, *Troilus ex Chaucero,* of which, however, there is no other record; [17] and in *The Rare Triumphes of Loue and Fortune,* which was "plaide before the Queenes most excellent Maiestie" about 1582 and published seven years later, the first of the plays given before the gods was that of "Troilus and Cressida," at the conclusion of which Mercury says:

> Behold, how Troilus and Cressida
> Cries out on Love, that framed their decay.[18]

How these plays treated Cressid it is useless to speculate. But in the popular literature of the early Tudor period she became a staple comparison while her uncle's name was becoming a common noun. Peculiarly enough, Cressid was often glorified as the highest type of a sweetheart,—

---

[17] Miss Spurgeon, vol. I, p. 95.

[18] Dodsley-Hazlitt's *Old Plays,* vol. VI, p. 155. This play reminds òne of the Troilus-Cressida burlesque—over which wars of words have been waged,—in *Histriomastix.* Nobody, I believe, has noticed that the latter is closely paralleled by this passage in Samuel Rowlands's *The Letting of Hvmovrs Blood in the Head-Vaine* . . . At London, Printed by W. White for W. F. 1600, signs. E *b*-E 2 (Hunterian Clùb edition, vol. I, pp. 66-67):

> My hartes deare blood sweete *Cis,* is thy carouse,
> Worth all the Ale in *Gammer Gubbins* house:
> I say no more affaires call me away,
> My Fathers horse for prouender doth stay.
> Be thou the Lady *Cressit-light* to mee,
> Sir *Trollelolle* I will proue to thee.
> Written in haste: farewell my Cowslippe sweete,
> Pray lets a Sunday at the Ale-house meete.

The early date of *Hvmovrs Blood* makes this passage of much importance in connection with the supposed allusion in *Histriomastix* to Shakespeare's *Troilus.*

as a complaisant damsel who "yielded grace" to her
lover's importunities, and who was worthy of emulation.
One could almost suspect that, tired with Chaucer's long-
drawn-out narrative, certain readers stopped at the great
climax in the third book of the *Troilus* and went on their
way, blissfully unaware of Criseyde's later perfidy. John
Skelton's poem, "To my lady Elisabeth Howarde"
(1523), uses Creisseid as a convenient means of compli-
menting Lady Elisabeth's beauty,[19] but the exaltation of
Cressid as a model mistress really begins with *Tottel's
Miscellany* (1557), where an unknown author is repre-
sented by a poem called "A comparison of his loue with
the faithfull and painful loue of *Troylus to Creside.*" [20]
He had evidently read Chaucer carefully through the third
book, for he borrows Chaucer's details freely. He tells
how Troilus fell in love with Creside at first sight, how
he was so hopelessly smitten that "euery ioye became a
wo," and how

> His chamber was his common walke,
> Wherin he kept him se[c]retely.
> He made his bedde the place of talke.

If the author had read all of the *Troilus,* he disregarded
the tragic *dénouement* for effect. After Creside had
granted her lover's wish, he says, she loved him faithfully
and studied "his whole minde full to content." He concludes by imploring his mistress

> To graunt me grace and so to do,
> As Creside then did Troylus to.

> And set me in as happy case,
> As Troylus with his lady was.

---

[19] *Works,* ed. A. Dyce, 1855, vol, II, p. 208. Cf. Miss Spurgeon, vol.
I, p. 74.
[20] Arber's reprint, pp. 192-194. There were eight editions of this
miscellany by 1587.

As a model lover Cresseda was depicted by William Elderton, the first noteworthy professional ballad-writer. In " The panges of Loue and louers fittes," his first known ballad, published on March 22, 1559/60, Elderton threw in a number of stock comparisons to romance and story, and wrote of Cresseda :

> Knowe ye not, how Troylus
> Languished and lost his joye,
> With fittes and fevers mervailous
> For Cresseda that dwelt in Troye;
> Tyll pytie planted in her brest,
>   Ladie ! ladie !
> To slepe with him, and graunt him rest,
>   My dear ladie.[21]

William Fulwood, a merchant-tailor who wrote a bitter though coarsely humorous satire on Elderton, published in 1568 *The Enimie of Idlenesse,* perhaps the first " complete letter-writer " in English. " The fourth Booke. Conteyning sundrie Letters belonging to love " contains a model poetical letter alluringly entitled " A constant Lover doth expresse His gripyng griefes, which still encrease," [22] the first few verses of which show a knowledge of Chaucer's story :

> As Troylus did neglect the trade of Lovers skilfull lawe,
> Before such time that Cresseid faire with fixed eyes he sawe,

and then plunges into a series of conventional comparisons—" But sith I lacke some such a friende as he of Pandor had . . ." and the like. The " letter " concludes with the plea :

---

[21] J. P. Collier's *Old Ballads*, p. 26 (Percy Society, vol. i). The ballad is reprinted also in H. L. Collmann's *Ballads and Broadsides*, Roxburghe Club, 1912, p. 111.

[22] Available to me only as reprinted (pp. 72-73) in Paul Wolter's *William Fullwood*, Diss. Rostock, Potsdam, 1907.

> Therfore graunt grace, as Cressida, did unto Troylus true:
> For as he had hir loue by right, so thine to me is due.

Cressida must have been held up as a worthy example by many young lover-writers, for the *Enimie of Idlenesse* went through eight editions by 1598.

The early Elizabethan poets, particularly Turbervile and Gascoigne, and ballad-mongers [23] of a much later period were fond of thus exalting Cressida. Poetic license, or licentiousness, was their only excuse, for her reputation had long been hopeless. In 1501 Gavin Douglas [24] casually referred to " Trew Troilus, vnfaithfull Cressida," as if these epithets had already become stereotyped; and in *Philip Sparrow* (1507) Skelton [25] summarized Chaucer's story, scoffed even at Troilus, and harshly expressed the general opinion of Cressida and Pandar:

> For she dyd but fayne;
> The story telleth playne . . .
> Thus in conclusyon,
> She brought hym in abusyon;
> In ernest and in game
> She was moch to blame;
> Disparaged is her fame,
> And blemysshed is her name,
> In maner half with shame;
> Troylus also hath lost
> On her moch loue and cost,
> And now must kys the post;
> Pandara, that went betwene,
> Hath won nothing, I wene . . .
> Yet for a speciall laud
> He is named Troylus baud,
> Of that name he is sure
> Whyles the world shall dure.

---

[23] See *A Handfull of Pleasant Delights*, 1584, Spenser Society edition, pp. 45, 56; Richard Johnson's *Crown Garland of Golden Roses*, 1612, Percy Society *Publications*, vol. VI, pp. 52, 67.

[24] *The Palice of Honour*, *Works*, ed. J. Small, 1874, vol. I, p. 23.

[25] *Works*, ed. Dyce, 1855, vol. I, pp. 84-85.

In the hands of "vulgar makers" Chaucer's story lent
itself admirably to burlesque. Skelton's own "doings"
(which, Puttenham gravely assures us, were always ridiculous) could only have added to Cressid's ill fame. But
worse was to come.

In 1565 a professional versifier wrote a coarsely humorous ballad on the lovers, which is preserved in a Bodleian
Library manuscript, famous because it contains the older
version of "Chevy Chase." [26] The ballad follows Chaucer
in every particular: Troilus thinks his heart is so per-
fectly under control that no beauty can allure him, but one
day at church he sees Cressyd. What a lurch did the sight

---

[26] *Songs and Ballads* . . . Edited from a MS. in the Ashmolean
Museum by Thomas Wright, Roxburghe Club, 1860, pp. 195-197.
The ballad is also reprinted in vol. XXXI, pp. 102-105, of the old
Shakespeare Society *Papers* by Halliwell-Phillipps as well as in his
edition of *Troilus* (Folio *Shakespeare*, vol. XII, p. 307). This is
almost certainly the "ballett intituled 'the history of Troilus,
Whose throtes [*i. e.*, troth] hath Well bene tryed'" which was
registered for publication by T. Purfoote in 1565-66 (Arber's *Transcript*, vol. I, p. 300).

Another ballad on Troilus and "Cressus," preserved in the *Percy
Folio MS.*, ed. Hales and Furnivall, vol. III, pp. 301-302, depends
solely on Chaucer's poem. It begins:

> Cressus: was the ffairest of Troye,
>   whom Troylus did loue!
> the K*n*i*gh*t was kind, & shee was coy,
>   no words nor worthes cold moue,
> till Pindaurus [!] soe playd his p*art*
> *tha*t the K*n*i*gh*t obtained her hart
>   the Ladyes rose destroyes:
> [They] held a sweet warr a winters night
> till the enuyous day gaue light;
>   wh*i*ch darkness louers ioyes.

It is most surprising that Henryson's story was not worked into
many lugubrious moralizing ballads of the type so dear to Elizabethan readers. One of these is mentioned on p. 24, below; and
probably there *were* others not now preserved.

give his heart! He is dismayed, and seeks the help of her uncle Pandarus. Pandar tells Cressyd that Troilus is dying for her love, though the young warrior nevertheless goes to the battlefield and gives the Greeks "many a lusty thwake-a." Cressyd, caught at her uncle's house by a rainstorm, is forced to pass the night there. Troilus goes to her chamber with Pandar, but is too tongue-tied to speak. He kneels by the bed, but Pandar places him in it, blows out the light, and leaves the two together. In the morning he returns.

> " In faythe, old unkell," then quoth she,
> " Yow are a frend to trust-a."
> Then Troylus lawghed, and wat you why?
> For he had what he lust-a.

Halliwell-Phillipps first commented on the resemblance of the ballad to Shakespeare's play. That resemblance is unmistakable, particularly in the characterization of Troilus,[27] who both in ballad and in drama is frankly sensual. It is by no means improbable that Shakespeare had heard this ballad sung about the streets of London,[28] and that alone would have given him a distaste for the love story: ballad-mongers and ballad-singers had made it coarse and farcical, and no Elizabethan poet would gladly, or willingly, have treated a theme which they had popularized and befouled.

Robert Henryson's *Testament of Creseyde* was published in Thynne's 1532 edition [29] of Chaucer, introduced

---

[27] Cf. especially *Troilus and Cressida*, IV, ii, 36-40.

[28] I have observed that one of the ballads in this MS. was registered in October, 1564, and yet was printed under Richard Johnson's name in his *Crown Garland*, 1612. The ballad on Troilus and Cressida could easily have been in circulation in Shakespeare's day.

[29] The quotations in this article are from Thynne's text (as normalized in Gregory Smith's *Henryson*, vol. III, pp. 177-198), because this was long the only text known in England. Otherwise the Scottish text (1593) would be preferable.

with the statement that " Thus endeth the fyfth and laste booke of Troylus : and here foloweth the pyteful and dolorous testament of fayre Creseyde," and concluding, " Thus endeth the pyteful and dolorous testament of fayre Creseyde : and here foloweth the legende of good women." The poem was probably written in the last quarter of the fifteenth century. The earliest record of it is in the table of contents of the British Museum MS. Asloan, *circâ* 1515, but the portion of the MS. which contained the poem is lost, and Thynne's is the earliest extant text. Perhaps Thynne did not intend it to be taken as Chaucer's work—Chaucer, indeed, is several times mentioned in the poem—but it was reprinted in all editions of Chaucer down to Urry's (1721), was attributed to him by Bale, Leland, and Tanner (1748), and was even included among his poems in Chalmers's *Works of the English Poets* (1810).[30] The oldest extant separate text is that published by Henry Charteris at Edinburgh in 1593. Six years after this, one of Francis Thynne's *Animadversions on Speght's Chaucer* was : " yt wolde be good that Chaucer's proper woorkes were distinguyshed from the adulterat, and suche as were not his, as the Testamente of Cressyde " ; [31] but in his 1602 edition Speght not only ignored this advice but inserted the following passage at the beginning of Chaucer's poem (folio 143) : " In this excellent Booke is shewed the feruent loue of Troylus to Creiseid, whome hee enioyed for a time : and her great vntruth to him againe in giuing her selfe to Diomedes, who in the end did so cast her off, that she came to great miserie. In which discourse Chaucer liberally treateth of the diuine purueiaunce."

---

[30] Henryson's *Works*, ed. Gregory Smith, Scottish Text Society, vol. I, p. xlv ff.

[31] Miss Spurgeon, vol. I, pp. 154-155.

Chaucer had confined himself to the tragi-comedy of Troilus, but the Scottish poet, on a cold winter night when he was reading the story "written by worthy Chaucer glorious," [32] perceived that inherent in the theme there was a real tragedy of Criseyde, a tragedy suggested by her own adjuration:

> And thou, Simoys, that as an arwe clere
> Thorugh Troye rennest ay downward to the see,
> Ber witnesse of this word that seyd is here,
> That thilke day that ich untrewe be
> To Troilus, myn owene herte free,
> That thou retorne bakwarde to thy welle,
> And I with body and soule sinke in helle! [33]

The continuation of the story, as Henryson wrote it, is the most artistic, the most powerful handling made by any poet after Chaucer. Animated no doubt by a desire to warn "worthy women" to "mynge nat your loue with false disception," he nevertheless wrote a genuinely dramatic poem, powerful in its delineation of character, gripping in the inevitability of its *dénouement,* and yet marked by the same sympathetic comprehension of the character of Creseyde that had made Chaucer pity her. The story could hardly end as Chaucer left it. There the ghost of Troilus looks down from the clouds upon the *comédie humaine* in which he had played such an unfortunate rôle and laughs at the pitiableness of his efforts and those of the living Trojans. But what of Criseyde? Was she true to Diomed? Could so sensual a man be true to her? Or was not his infatuation a mere whim caused by a desire of showing his superiority to her Trojan lover? Henryson's beautiful story answers all these questions in a manner

---

[32] The allusions to Chaucer in the *Testament* are, of course, in Miss Spurgeon's book (vol. I, p. 56).

[33] *Troilus and Criseyde*, Bk. IV, st. 222.

that is beyond praise—with the sure touch of an artist. But in doing so he rang Criseyde's " bell " so loudly that it reverberated to the time of Shakespeare, and forever damned her as a loose woman.

The Diomedes Chaucer portrayed could not possibly have been true to Criseyde: once he had gained her body, once he had triumphed over the lover Troilus, Criseyde could no longer attract him. Henryson knew this. And he was entirely unfamiliar with the courtly-love rules that had motivated Chaucer's treatment of Criseyde, but instead regarded her as a wanton even in her relations with Troilus and as the kept mistress of Diomedes.[34] Accord-

---

[34] So thought also Sir Francis Kinaston, who *circâ* 1635 began to translate *Troilus* into Latin and pointed out that the " Sixt & Last Booke of Troilus and Creseid " was not by Chaucer but by " Mr. Robert Henderson,"—surprising news to most of his contemporaries. " This Mr Henderson," he said, " wittily obseruing that Chaucer in his 5th booke had related the death of Troilus, but made no mention what became of Creseid, he learnedly takes vppon him in a fine poeticall way to expres the punishment & end due to a false vnconstant whore, which commonly terminates in extreme misery " (G. Smith's *Henryson*, vol. I, p. ciii; cf. also Miss Spurgeon, vol. I, p. 207). Both Henryson and Kinaston were quite modern in their attitude toward Cressid.

Ballad-mongers naturally took an unfavorable view of Cressid's relations with Troilus. So " A Ballade in Praise of London Prentices, and What They Did at the Cock-Pitt Playhouse " (Collier's *Hist. Eng. Dramatic Poetry*, 1879, vol. I, p. 387), of the date of March, 1616/7, tells us that

> King Priam's robes were soon in rags,
> And broke his gilded scepter;
> False Cressid's hood, that was so good
> When loving Troylus kept her. . . .

The ballad, if genuine, perhaps throws some light on the way in which actors played the part of Cressid. The author of " A New Ballad of King Edward and Jane Shore," 1671 (*Roxburghe Ballads*, vol. VIII, p. 424), is quite as uncomplimentary to " young Troyalus " as his predecessors were to Cressid.

ingly, he tells us that it was not long before Diomedes tired
of Creseyde and drove her out. It grieves him to be forced
to admit that

> Than desolate she walked vp and downe,
> As, some men sayne, in the courte as commune.[35]

Finally she returns to Calchas. Going into a private ora-
tory of the temple, she bitterly reproaches Venus and
Cupid for the evils they have sent on her; and falling
asleep, dreams that her case is being tried by the gods, that
Venus is demanding punishment for her impiety, that the
gods decree her offence punishable by leprosy. Cynthia
and Saturn descend to deliver the verdict. And a fearful
one it is!

> Thy christal eyen menged with blode I make;
> Thy voice so clere, vnplesaunt, heer, and hace;
> Thy lusty lere ouerspred with spottes blake,
> And lumpes hawe appering in thy face;
> Where thou comest, eche man shal flye the place;
> Thus shalte thou go beggyng fro house to hous,
> With cuppe and clapper lyke a lazarous.[36]

Creseyde awakes to find that her dream has come true.
She leaves the temple secretly with her father, and goes to
the "spyttel house," where only a few lepers recognize her.
She moans and cries, but finally is reconciled to begging.
One day Troilus, riding by, is reminded by her terrible
eyes of his lost lady-love, and impetuously pours money
and jewels into her dish. Creseyde is frantic with grief.
Feeling death approaching, she requests one of the lepers
to carry her ruby ring to Troilus and to tell him of her un-
happy end. When Troilus receives the ring and hears the
message, he is filled with agony. But, alas! what can he
do? She has been untrue to him—he can only furnish the

---

[35] Ll. 76-77.   [36] Ll. 337-343.

grave in which the lepers have hastily buried her with a splendid monument and think of her! A beautiful and a pitiful story!

It should be obvious that most readers took the *Testament* for Chaucer's own work. In the third and fourth lines Henryson does say, "whan I began to write this tragedy," but that statement could easily be overlooked because of what follows, and besides the poem was unsigned. It was a stormy, cold night, Henryson says; I mended the fire, took a drink to arm me from the cold, opened a book written by glorious Chaucer, in which I read the story of fair Creseyde and Troilus,—of how Troilus nearly died of grief when he was forsaken. And then

> To breke my slepe another queare I toke,
> In whiche I founde the fatal desteny
> Of fayre Creseyde, whiche ended wretchedly.
>
> Who wot if al that Chaucer wrate was trewe?
> Nor I wotte nat if this narration
> Be authorysed, or forged of the newe,
> Of some poete, by his inuention.[37]

This " other queare " could easily have been mistaken for a continuation of the story by Chaucer. Perhaps in the verses just quoted Henryson was trying to give that impression.[38] At any rate, the stanza form, the smoothly flowing verse (which probably sounded smoother and more regular to the Elizabethan ear than did Chaucer's own), the attitude towards the characters,—these might well have been thought Chaucer's. And the inevitability of Henryson's *dénouement,* even though it necessitated the resur-

[37] Ll. 61-67.

[38] Professor Skeat thought that these lines threw some doubt on Henryson's authorship. Cf. his *Chaucerian and Other Pieces,* p. 522.

rection of Troilus, should have removed all doubts of the authenticity of the poem.

Henryson made his Creseyde a life-like, suffering woman, struck down in the height of her folly by inexorable retribution. For authors and for readers up to 1600 Henryson's Cressid was *the* Cressid; but lacking his sympathy, they regarded her as a light-of-love who finally paid for her faithlessness and unchastity by leprosy. The influence of Henryson on the story was immense. He completely diverted it from the channel in which Chaucer had left it; but, nevertheless, every mention of Cressid as a leper, at least to 1600, is an allusion to Chaucer. People thought they were reading Chaucer: nobody had ever heard of Robert Henryson, schoolmaster.

Nor did Elizabethan writers have any idea of the origin of the Cressid myth, although many of them knew Boccaccio's " tragedies." A ballad registered at Stationers' Hall in 1564-65 and preserved in a Bodleian Library manuscript [39] begins,

> In Bocas an Guydo I rede and fynde,
> Thatt wemen of verrey nature and kynde,
> Be subtyll and unstedfaste of mynde,

but shows no knowledge of Guido's or Boccaccio's Cressid. George Turbervile translated some of Boccaccio's tales, constantly quotes him, and mentions him in connection with Chaucer, but knew Troilus and Cressid only as they appeared in Chaucer's works. In his *Epitaphes, Epigrams, Songs and Sonets* (1567) Turbervile devotes a poem to the story of Briseis, Chryseis, and the Wrath of

---

[39] Registered, I have observed, under the title of its refrain, " I will say nothing," in 1564-65 (Arber's *Transcript*, vol. I, p. 270); printed in Thomas Wright's *Songs and Ballads*, Roxburghe Club, 1860, p. 163.

Achilles; [40] if he had actually read the *Iliad,* he must have observed that a Pandarus plays an important rôle in Books iv-v and that Briseis, in Book xix, is described as a Trojan widow. But Turbervile, though deeply impressed by Chaucer's and Henryson's narratives, perceived no connection between Briseis and Cressid, and probably derived his information about Achilles, Briseis, and Chryseis, only from Ovid's *Epistles,* which, in 1567 (or earlier), he had translated. His poems are literally full of allusions to the Troilus-Cressida story, which he constantly uses in his doleful love ditties, as a fearful warning to obdurate and faithless mistresses. On one occasion " Finding his Mistresse vntrue, he exclaimeth thereat " [41] as follows:

> Farewell thou shamelesse shrew,
>   faire Cresides heire thou art:
> And I Sir Troylus earst haue been,
>   as prooueth by my smart.
> Hencefoorth beguile the Greekes,
>   no Troyans will thee trust:
> I yeeld thee vp to Diomed,
>   to glut his filthie lust.

But the Henryson story was always in Turbervile's mind. " The Lover in vtter dispaire of his Ladies returne,

---

[40] In J. P. Collier's reprint of the *Epitaphes,* pp. 223-226. On p. 10 occurs this little known allusion to Chaucer and Boccaccio:

> Pause, pen, a while therefore,
>   and use thy woonted meane:
> For Boccas braine, and Chaucers quill
>   in this were foyled cleane.
> Of both might neither boast
>   if they did live againe;
> For P[yndara]. would put them to their shifts
>   to pen hir vertues plaine.

[41] In *Tragical Tales, translated by Tvrbervile, In time of his troubles,* 1587 (Edinburgh reprint, 1837, p. 330). The *Tales,* as I shall prove elsewhere, was first printed in 1574-75.

in eche respect compares his estate with Troylus," a poem
in the *Épitaphes* (p. 249), brims with allusions to Chaucer's own poem but concludes with this characteristic
passage, which borrows both details and phrases from
Henryson:

> But though my fortune frame awrie,
> And I, dispoylde hir companie,
> Must waste the day and night in wo,
> For that the gods appointed so,
> I naythelesse will wish hir well
> And better than to Cresid fell:
> I pray she may have better hap
> Than beg hir bread with dish and clap,
> As shee, the sielie miser, did,
> When Troylus by the spittle rid.
> God shield hir from the lazars lore,
> And lothsome leapers stincking sore,
> And for the love I earst hir bare
> I wish hir as my selfe to fare.

The poet was not always so charitable. " To his cruel Mistresse," [42] at another time, he frankly remarks:

---

[42] *Ibid.*, p. 369. On p. 334 we read:

> When Cresid clapt the dish,
>   and Lazer-like did goe:
> She rewde no doubt that earst she did
>   the Troyan handle so.
> And might she then retirde
>   to beuties auncient towre:
> She would haue stucke to Priams sonne,
>   of faithful loue the floure.
> But fond, too late she found
>   that she had been too light:
> And ouerlate bewaild that she
>   forewent the worthy knight.

So in the *Epitaphes,* 1567 (Collier's reprint, pp. 108-109):

> Let Creside be in coumpt
>   and number of the mo,
> Who for hir lightnesse may presume
>   with falsest on the row;

And if I may not haue
　　the thing I would enioy:
　I pray the gods to plague thee
　　as they did the dame of Troy.
I meane that Creside coy
　　that linkt her with a Greeke:
And left the lusty Troyan Duke,
　　of all his loue to seeke.
And so they wil, I trust,
　　a mirror make of thee:
That beuties darlings may beware,
　　when they thy scourge shal see!

The enormous popularity of Turbervile's poems, doggerel though most of them are, helped to make the name of Cressid odious, or worse, comical.

Thomas Howell's " The britlenesse of thinges mortall, and the trustinesse of Vertue," a poem in spasmodic rime royal published in his *Newe Sonets, and pretie Pamphlets* (*circâ* 1570),[43] is so important for this discussion and so

Else would she not have left
　　a Trojan for a Greeke.
But what? by kinde the cat will hunt;
　　hir father did the like.

There are similar long allusions on pp. 54, 56-57. The *Epitaphes* was issued in ?1565, 1567, 1570, 1579, 1584. Turbervile had a brother and various nephews and cousins named Troilus (Hutchins, *History and Antiquities of Dorset*, 3rd edition, vol. I, pp. 139, 201), but whether there were likewise Cressids in the family, the record telleth not!

[43] Originally licensed in 1567-68, but no copy of the first edition remains. The present edition claims to be " newly augmented, corrected and amended. Imprinted at London in Flete-streete, at the signe of S. Iohn Euangelist, by Thomas Colwell." Colwell's last license (for a ballad) was secured in July, 1571 (Arber's *Transcript*, vol. I, p. 444); he is last heard of in a marginal note beside the entry of a book he had registered in 1568-9: "solde to Benyman, 19 Junij 1573 " (Arber, vol. I, p. 378); so that Howell's *Newe Sonets* probably appeared about 1570. Grosart, reprinting the second edition, does not attempt to date it. Miss Spurgeon, vol. I,

inaccessible as to deserve quotation. Four stanzas of the
poem deal with Cressid:

> Where is faire *Helines* bewtie now be come,
> Or *Cressed* eke whom *Troylus* long time serued,
> Where be the decked daintie Dame of Rome,
> That in Aurelius time so flourished:
> As these and many mo are vanished,
> So shall your youth, your fauor, and your grace,
> When nothing els but vertue may take place.
>
> To vertue therfore do your selues applie,
> Cale *Cressids* lyfe vnto your youthly minde,
> Who past her time in *Troye* most pleasauntly
> Till falsinge faith to vice she had inclinde
> For whiche to hir suche present plagues were sinde,
> That she in Lazers lodge her life did ende,
> Which wonted was most choysly to be tende.
>
> Hir comly corpes that *Troylus* did delight
> All puft with plages full lothsomly there lay:
> Hir Azurde vaines, her Cristall skinne so whight,
> With Purple spots, was falne in great decay:
> Hir wrinkeled face once fayre doth fade away,
> Thus she abode plagde in midst of this hir youth,
> Was forst to beg for breaking of hir truth.

After having thus paraphrased Henryson, the last stanza,
with unconscious irony, continues the denunciation with
an imitation of Chaucer's phraseology:

> Lo here the ende of wanton wicked life,
> Lo here the fruit that Sinne both sowes and reapes;
> Lo here of vice the right rewarde and knife,
> That cutth of cleane and tombleth downe in heapes,
> All such as treadeth Cresids cursed steps,
> Take heede therefore how you your youthes do spende,
> For vice bringes plagues, and vertue happie ende.[44]

---

p. 10u, merely refers to the work under its original date. But cf.
Herbert-Ames, *Typographical Antiquities*, II, p. 932.

[44] *The Poems of Thomas Howell*, ed. A. B. Grosart, pp. 121-122.
Cf. Chaucer's *Troilus*, Bk. v, st. 262, 265.

In 1581 Howell published his *Deuises, for his owne exercise, and his Friends pleasure,*[45] and there included this poem, changing the title to "Ruine the rewarde of Vice," considerably recasting all the verses, and adding a stanza. It is very probable that Shakespeare knew Howell's *Deuises,* and he could hardly have accused Howell of writing maliciously of Cressid. It cannot be insisted too often that readers of the *Testament* thought they were reading Chaucer. "Chaucers woorkes bee all printed in one volume," John Fox wrote in 1570, "and therfore knowen to all men." [46] But if all men had read that volume, they also had the idea of Cressid that Howell has here expressed.

George Gascoigne was fascinated by the Troilus-Cressid story, and refers to it with persistent and monotonous reiteration. The *Posies* (1575), his ungainly collection of plays and poems, mentions the lovers on nearly every page! Miss Spurgeon [47] quotes these verses from "Dan Bartholmew his first Triumphe":

> Thy brother *Troylus* eke, that gemme of gentle deedes,
> To thinke howe he abused was, alas, my heart it bleedes!
> He bet about the bushe, whiles other caught the birds,
> Whome crafty *Cresside* mockt to muche, yet fed him still with
>   words.
> And God he knoweth, not I, who pluckt hir first-sprong rose,
> Since *Lollius* and *Chaucer* both make doubt vpon that glose.

The mention of Lollius is important as showing that Gascoigne had read *Troilus* with some care but that he knew nothing of its source in Boccaccio,—a fact which, in the light of his knowledge of Italian, is a bit surprising. Miss

---

[45] In Grosart's edition. A separate edition was edited by Sir Walter Raleigh, Oxford, 1906.
[46] Miss Spurgeon, vol. I, p. 105.
[47] *Ibid.,* p. 110.

Spurgeon omits the four lines that directly follow those above:

> But this I knowe to well, and he to farre it felte,
> How *Diomede* vndid his knots, & caught both brooch and belt,
> And how she chose to change, and how she changed still,
> And how she dyed leaper-like, against hir louers will.

Gascoigne's information about Cressid's unchastity, then, came primarily from the *Testament*. Henryson's Creseyde's last words were:

> " O Diomede! thou hast both broohe & belte,
>   Whiche Troylus gaue me in tokenyng
>   Of his trewe loue "—& with that worde she swelte;[48]

---

[48] Ll. 579-581. The belt is Henryson's addition. The Scottish poet Wedderburne (*Bannatyne MS.*, 1568, ed. Hunterian Club, vol. IV, p. 761; Sibbald's *Chron. Scot. Poetry*, vol. III, p. 236), following both Henryson and Chaucer, piles an alarming assortment of articles on the weapon of Diomedes:

> God wait quhat wo had Troyelus in deid,
> Quhen he beheld the belt, the broch and ring,
> Hingand vpoun the speir of Diomeid,
> Quhilk Troyellus gaif to Cresseid in luve taikning.

This last line is almost an exact quotation of Henryson, ll. 500-501 (quoted above). But Wedderburne, like his English contemporaries, thought he was quoting Chaucer. In this same poem there is a stanza (unnoticed by Miss Spurgeon) in which he summarizes the *Miller's Tale*.

The limits of this article necessarily preclude an attempt to trace the story through the Scottish poets. A remarkable poem, "The Laste Epistle of Creseyd to Troyalus," attributed to William Fowler (*Works*, vol. I, pp. 379-387, ed. H. W. Meikle, 1914), should be mentioned, however. This aims to finish Henryson's poem, and does so by borrowing his situation and retelling the whole story of the *Testament* plus details presumably from Lydgate and certainly from Chaucer. The date of this poem is, I should guess, about 1603, when Fowler came to London with Queen Anne. (The second volume of Meikle's edition has not appeared, and he has not expressed his opinion.) At any rate, Fowler was unaware of, or totally unimpressed by, Shakespeare's play.

and this explains the persistent allusions in Elizabethan poems to " brooch and belt."

In " Dan Bartholmewes Dolorous discourses " Gascoigne writes:

> I found naught else but tricks of *Cressides* kinde,
> Which playnly proude that thou weart of hir bloud.
> I found that absent *Troylus* was forgot,
> When *Dyomede* had got both brooch and belt,
> Both gloue and hand, yea harte and all, God wot,
> When absent *Troylus* did in sorowes swelt,[49]

and then concludes by imitating Chaucer's epilogue to the *Troilus:* [50]

> Lo, here the cause for why I take this payne!
> Lo, how I loue the wight which me doth hate!
> Lo, thus I lye, and restlesse rest in Bathe. . . .[51]

In another passage Gascoigne remarks:

> And saye as *Troylus* sayde, since that I can no more,
> Thy wanton wyll dyd wauer once, and woe is me therefore,[52]

almost an exact rendering of Henryson's lines (591-592). Such examples, and more could easily be cited, show clearly that Gascoigne made no distinction between Chaucer's poem and Henryson's. On the contrary, they prove that, at least from Gascoigne's point of view, his allusions to Cressid's leprosy are allusions to Chaucer.[53]

George Whetstone, in the *Rocke of Regard* (1576), was,

---

[49] *Complete Poems*, ed. Hazlitt, vol. I, p. 114.
[50] Bk. v, st. 262, 265. Cf. Howell, p. 404, *supra*.
[51] Hazlitt's ed., vol. I, p. 115.
[52] *Ibid.*, vol. I, p. 90. Henryson's lines are:

> Sigheng ful sadly, sayde, "I can no more;
> She was vntrewe, and wo is me therfore!"

[53] Similar allusions may be found in Hazlitt's edition, vol. I, pp. 54, 55, 92, 98, 101, 105-106, 133, 139, 140, 363, 493, 495, and elsewhere.

perhaps even more than Gascoigne, influenced by Henryson, and is extremely severe on poor Cressid, frankly announcing in his preface " To all the young Gentlemen of England " that in *Cressids Complaint,* the title of one poem in the first division of his book, " the subtilties of a courtisan discovered may forwarne youth from the companie of inticing dames." " The Argument for Cressids complaint," quoted below, shows to what a sad state Henryson's poem had brought the reputation of Cressid, making her, in Whetstone's eyes, a strumpet even while she was carrying on her love affair with Troilus :

> The inconstancie of Cressid is so readie in every mans mouth, as it is a needelesse labour to blase at full her abuse towards yong Troilus, her frowning on Syr Diomede, her wanton lures and love: neverthelesse, her companie scorned, of thousandes sometimes sought, her beggerie after braverie, her lothsome leprosie after lively beautie, her wretched age after wanton youth, and her perpetuall infamie after violent death, are worthy notes (for others heede) to be remembred. And for as much as Cressids heires in every corner live, yea, more cunning then Cressid her selfe in wanton exercises, toyes and inticements, to forewarne all men of such filthes, to persuade the infected to fall from their follies, and to rayse a feare in dames untainted to offend, I have reported the subtile sleites, the leaud life, and evill fortunes of a courtisane, in Cressid[s] name; whom you may suppose, in tattered weedes, halfe hungerstarved, miserably arrayde, with scabs, leprosie, and mayngie, to complaine as followeth.[54]

In the complaint itself, which ironically enough is written in rime royal, Cressid frankly admits that she was always a wanton, that she deliberately enticed Troilus and was all the while prostituting her body to other Trojans. She refers to " Syr Chaucer " [55] (which shows that Whetstone wrote the piece with Chaucer's Criseyde in mind), but borrows all her woes (including, of course, " the brooch

[54] *Rocke of Regard,* J. P. Collier's reprint, p. 35.
[55] *Ibid.,* p. 39 (Miss Spurgeon, vol. I, p. 113).

and belt" which Diomedes got) from Henryson. Where Creseyde has said:

> This leper loge take for thy goodly bour,
> And for thy bedde take nowe a bonch of stro;
> Far wayled wyne and meates thou had tho,
> Take mouled breed, pirate, and syder sour:
> But cuppe and clapper, nowe is al ago,[56]

Whetstone's Cressid cries,—

> Glad is she now a browne breade crust to gnawe,
> Who, deintie once, on finest cates did frowne;
> To couch upon soft seames a pad of straw,
> Where halfe mislikt were stately beds of downe:
> By neede enforst, she begs on every clowne
> On whom but late the best would gifts bestow;
> But squemish then, God dyld ye, she said no.[57]

The Epilogue imitates Chaucer's conclusion in the same fashion as Howell and Gascoigne had earlier done:

> Loe! here the fruits of lust and lawlesse love,
> Loe! here their faults that vale to either vice;
> Loe! ladyes, here their falles (for your behove)
> Whose wanton willes sets light by sound advice.
> Here lords may learn with noble dames to match;
> For dunghill kyte from kinde will never flye. . . .[58]

Surely if Dr. Furnivall had read *Cressids Complaint* he would never have said that we owe Shakespeare a grudge for debasing Chaucer's beautiful story! The grudge, if one be owed, must be against Henryson, while Shakespeare deserves our thanks for pulling Cressid partly out of the mire in which Henryson's followers had placed her.

---

[56] Ll. 433-437.

[57] Collier's reprint, p. 40. Thomas Deloney's ballad of "Jane Shore" (*Works*, ed. F. O. Mann, p. 304, st. 9-11) seems to be imitating both Whetstone and Henryson, though the resemblance is probably accidental. Whetstone has other allusions to Cressid on pp. 134, 279. Cf. also his mention of Achilles and Briseis on p. 140.

[58] Collier's reprint, p. 91.

Sabia, in *Common Conditions* (before 1576), replies to Nomides's question, " What constancy in *Creseda* did rest in euery thinge ? " thus:

> How faythfull was *Deomedes* one of the *Greekishe* crew
> Though *Troilus* therin was iust yet was hee found vntrewe.
> And so betweene those twaine, and fortunes luckles hap,
> Shee was like Lazer faine to sit and beg with dish and clap.[59]

The allusions were no doubt understood and appreciated by every audience. From 1575 to 1585 poetical miscellanies, under fantastic and verbose titles, swarmed; and Cressid's name monotonously appears in them, along with that of Helen, as a fearful example. Cressid, however, is only once referred to in *The Paradyse of daynty deuises* (1576): there a certain R. L. has occasion to illustrate his remarks by the story of Medea and Jason. He then writes:

> Vnto whose grace yelde he, as I doe offer me,
> Into your hands to haue his happ, not like hym for to be:
> But as kyng Priamus [?sonne], did binde hym to the will,
> Of Cressed false whiche hym forsoke, with Diomed to spill.
>
> So I to you commende my faithe, and eke my ioye,
> I hope you will not bee so false, as Cressed was to Troye:
> For if I bee vntrue, her Lazares death I wishe,
> And eke in thee if thou bee false, her clapper and her dishe.[60]

The *Gorgious Gallery of gallant Inuentions* (1578) is crowded with allusions to Henryson's Cressid. One lover, who is quite as ungallant as R. L., " writeth to his Lady a desperate Farewell," and remarks:

Thy fawning flattering wordes, which now full falce I finde,
Perswades mee to content my selfe, and turne from *Cressids* kinde.

---

[59] *Common Conditions*, ed. Tucker Brooke, 1915, ll. 801, 820-823. See also l. 1281.

[60] " Beyng in Loue, he complaineth," J. P. Collier's reprint of 1578 edition of the *Paradyse*, p. 132. There were eight editions by 1600.

And all the sorte of those: that vse such craft I wish
A speedy end, or lothsome life, to liue with *Lasars* dish.[61]

Another lover, exhorting " his Lady to bee constant," reminds her that

> The fickle are blamed:
> Their lightiloue shamed,
> Theyr foolishnesse doth make them dye:
> As well,
> Can *Cressid* beare witnesse,
> Fordge of her owne distresse,
> Whom Leprosy paynted
> And penury taynted.[62]

More intelligent use of Henryson's narrative is made by
A poore Knight his Pallace of priuate pleasures (1579),
an elaborate allegory. Morpheus escorts the poor knight
to the Vale of Venus, where among other unfortunate
lovers he sees Troilus and Cressid:

> And as I pryed by chaunce, I saw a damsell morne,
> With ragged weedes, and Lazers spots, a wight to much forlorne.
> Quoth *Morpheus* doost thou see, wheras that caytiffe lyes,
> Much like the wretched *Crocodill*, beholde now how shee cryes.
> That is *Pandare* his Nice, and *Calcas* only childe,
> By whose deceites and pollicies, young *Troylus* was beguilde.
> Shee is kept in affliction where many other are,
> And veweth *Troylus* lying dead, vpon the Mount of *Care*.
> Shee wepte, shee sighed, she sobd, for him shee doth lament,
> And all too late, yet to to vaine, her facte shee doth repent:
> How could that stedfast knight, (quoth I) loue such a dame?
> *Morpheus* replied in beauty bright, shee bare away the fame:
> Till that shee had betrayd, her *Troylus* and her dere,
> And then the Gods assigned a plague, and after set her here.[63]

---

[61] Sign. C *b* (*Three Collections of English Poetry*, ed. Sir Henry
Ellis, London, 1845).

[62] Sign. E iii *b* (*ibid.*) Similar allusions may be found at signs.
B ii *b*, B iii, E ii *b*, F iii *b*, G iv *b*, H ii, K iii *b*, and elsewhere.

[63] Sign. B iiii *b* (Ellis's *Three Collections*). The phrase " *Pandor
his Neece* " is used again at sign. D ii *b*, and of course comes only
from Chaucer's story.

The poor knight, indeed, seems to have read the *Testament
of Creseyde* with more attention than most of his fellow
writers. He noticed, for instance, that while Creseyde had
bequeathed her " corse and caryoun With wormes and with
toodes to be rent," she had also said:

> My spirite I leaue to Diane, wher she dwelles,
> To walke with her in waste wodes & welles; [64]

and accordingly, in another poem, he puts her in the train
of Diana. Cupid's army approaches, and Desire is sent to
demand Diana's surrender. This is refused. Desire returns to Cupid, and is ordered to ambush the maidens. He
does so, and " when as worthy *Troylus* came, how could
Dame *Cressid* fight ? " But this was no prelude to a happy
reunion in the Other World. The poor knight was too
prejudiced for that, and hastened to add:

> But rather then Dame *Cressid* would, so quickly seeme as dead,
> Shee vowed her selfe from *Troylus* true, to flattering *Diomede.*
> So that the periured *Grecian,* or els the *Troyan* knight,
> Should haue Dame *Cressid* vnto loue, yea both if so it might. [65]

In " Iustice and Iudgement, pleaded at Beauties Barre,"
the poor knight devotes five stanzas (in rime royal) to
Cressid. [66] All the gods and Venus sit beside Beauty, and
after Helen has been condemned and led away, Troilus
offers his bill of complaint against Cressid. Diomedes tries

---

[64] Ll. 577-578.   [65] Sign. D iii *b.*
[66] Signs. F-F *b.* Cf. also sign. I iii. In W. A.'s *Speciall Remedie
against the furious force of lawlesse Loue,* 1579 (reprinted in Ellis's
Three Collections), sign. F ii *b,* there is a rather interesting reference
to Cressid:

What madnesse then remaines, in mens vnruly mindes,
  to feede one fruits of vaine desire, ye which so soone vntwindes[?]
For wher is now become, dame *Cressids* glorious hue,
  whose passing port, so much did please, young Troilus eyes to vew?
W. A., of course, is alluding to the leprosy story.

to defend her, but is routed by Troilus; Calchas offers
" glistering gobs of gold " if Beauty will spare her; but
Beauty would not

giue eare, vnto the tale hee tolde,
But iudged her which was the Prophets daughter
A Leper vile, and so shee liued after.

Here a new twist ha's been given to the story, though the
author was indebted to Henryson for his idea. He has
simply paraphrased the description of Creseyde's dream as
given by the Scottish poet.

On June 23, 1581, Edward White licensed " A proper
ballad Dialoge wise betwene Troylus and Cressida," which
wa's probably, I think, a reprint of a ballad in two parts—
" A Complaint " (by " Troilus ") and " A Replye " (by
" Cressida ")—that had been published in the 1580 edi-
tion of the *Paradyse of daynty deuises*.[67] The " Com-
plaint " is a bitter attack in which Troilus laments that
Cressida's " gadding moode " ca'used her to be unfaithful.
" If she in *Troy* had tarryed still," the ballad-writer makes
Troilus say,

She had not knoune the Lazars call,
With cuppe & clap her almes to winne:
Nor how infective scabbe and scall,
Do cloth the Lepre Ladies skinne: [68]
She had no such distresse in *Troy*,
But honor, favour, wealth, and ioy.

In the " Replye " Cressida denies that a " gadding moode,
but forced strife " took her from Troy: if Troilus had only
made her his wife, they might have lived happily together.
As it is, she a'sks for pity, not blame; and grieves because

---

[67] Edited by Sir E. Brydges, 1812, pp. 100-102. Published also in
Gascoigne's *Poems*, ed. W. C. Hazlitt, vol. II, pp. 331-333.

[68] This absurd phrase may come from Henryson, l. 464: " a leper
lady rose, and to her wende."

Troilus is " blazing " her " plague to make it more." In the *Testament* Troilus is profoundly touched by the resemblance of the leper to Cressid, and almost dies of grief when he discovers that the leper *was* Cressid. Such a production as this ballad, then, keeps neither to the spirit of Henryson nor of Chaucer, but the ballad-writer was reflecting the popular idea of the unfortunate woman.

" The Louer complaineth the losse of his Ladie," a ballad by I. Thomson in *A Handefull of pleasant delites* (1584),[69] combines details from the *Troilus* and the *Testament* in this fashion:

> If *Venus* would grant vnto me,
>   such happinesse:
> As she did vnto *Troylus*,
> By help of his friend *Pandarus*,
>   To *Cressids* loue who worse,
>   Than all the women certainly:
>   That euer liued naturally.
> Whose slight falsed faith, the storie saith,
> Did breed by plagues, her great and sore distresse,
>   For she became so leprosie,
>   That she did die in penurie:
>   Because she did transgresse.[70]

The " storie " to which Thomson refers was, of course, the six books of *Troilus and Criseyde* as printed by Thynne.

Robert Greene, in *Euphues his censure to Philautus* (1587), introduces Iphigenia, Briseis, and Cressida, as three Greek ladies who frequently meet with Cassandra,

---

[69] That the *Handfull of Pleasant Delights* first appeared in 1566, as an entry in the Stationers' Registers for that year (Arber's *Transcript*, vol. I, p. 313) would naturally lead one to expect, and that most of the ballads printed in the 1584 *Handfull* had actually been published before 1566, I have attempted to prove in an article presently to appear in the *Journal of English and Germanic Philology*.

[70] *A Handefull*, etc., Spenser Society edition, p. 32. Henryson does not mention Pandarus.

Polyxena, Andromache, and the Greek and Trojan warriors to discuss philosophy and literature,—all these personages being sublimely unconscious that the works they are discussing were not to be written for hundreds of years. Mr. C. H. Herford has suggested [71] that this anachronism may have led Shakespeare into putting Aristotle's philosophy in Hector's mouth. Certainly in the *Winter's Tale* Shakespeare followed Greene by giving Bohemia a sea-coast—an error that aroused the scornful ridicule of Ben Jonson. In the "third discourse" Greene speaks of "*Cressida,* who all that night had smoothered in hir thoughts the perfection of *Troilus*," [72] but a remark of his Orlando Furioso,—

Why strumpet, worse than Mars his trothlesse loue.
Falser than faithles Cressida: strumpet thou shalt not scape,—[73]

shows that his opinion of Cressida was hardly favorable.

With *Willobie His Avisa. Or The true Picture of a modest Maid, and of a chast and constant wife* (1594) we come close to Shakespeare. In her "Second Temptation . . . after her marriage by Ruffians, Roysters, young Gentlemen, and lustie Captaines, which all shee quickly cuts off," the impossible Avisa, out-Susaning Susanna, delivers this crushing retort to her tempters:

Though shamelesse Callets may be found;
That Soyle them selves in common field;
And can carire the whoores rebound,
To straine at first, and after yeeld:
Yet here are none of *Creseds* kind,
In whome you shall such fleeting find.[74]

---

[71] In his *Works of Shakespeare* (1902), vol. III, pp. 359-60.
[72] Greene's *Prose Works*, ed. A. B. Grosart, vol. VI, p. 233.
[73] *Historie of Orlando Furioso*, Malone Society reprint, ll. 1065-66. For similar slurs see Greene's *Never Too Late*, 1590, *Prose Works*, ed. Grosart, vol. VIII, pp. 26, 59, 68.
[74] Ed. Charles Hughes, 1904, Canto XVIII, p. 51.

Willobie himself then assailed the constant dame, only to be told in " Avisa, her last reply,"

> Assure your selfe, you know my mind,
> My hart is now, as first it was,
> I came not of dame *Chrysiedes* kind.[75]

To the *Avisa* is added a poem called " The praise of a contented mind," in which Willobie shows that Henryson was his chief authority for the Cressid story. He writes:

> For carelesse Crysed that had gin, her hand, her faith and hart,
> To Troilus her trustie friend, yet falsely did depart:
> And giglotlike from Troye towne, to Grecians campe would goe,
> To Diomede, whom in the end, she found a faithless foe.
> For having sliu'd the gentle slip, his love was turnd to hate.
> And she a leaper did lament, but then it was too late.
> Now foolish fancie was the cause, this Crysed did lament,
> For when she had a faithfull friend, she could not be content.[76]

Sir Sidney Lee [77] believes that Shakespeare was the Mr. W. S., an old player, referred to in the *Avisa;* but whether or not this be true, Shakespeare probably noticed the book because he was actually mentioned by name in the prefatory verses. His opinion of Cressida was exactly the same as that of Master Willobie.

By 1596, the year in which Thomas Heywood's *Iron Age* seems to have first been played,[78] Cressid's features

---

[75] Ed. Hughes, p. 133, Canto LXXII.

[76] *Ibid.*, pp. 138-139. The third verse is a rendering of Henryson's " And go among the grekes early and late, So gyglotlyke, takyng thy foule plesaunce " (ll. 82-83). The ugly phrase in the first half of the fifth line is also used by Gascoigne, *Poems*, ed. Hazlitt, vol. I, p. 105.

[77] *Life of Shakespeare* (1916), pp. 219-221.

[78] *Troy* was entered in Henslowe's *Diary* (ed. Greg, vol. II, p. 180) as a new play on June 22, 1596, and was performed five or six times during June and July (*ibid.*, vol. I, p. 42). Greg (*ibid.*, vol. II, p. 180) thinks that this was an earlier and shorter part of the *Iron Age*, which was later expanded into a two-part play. The *Iron Age* was first published in 1632; in the preface to the two parts Heywood

were fixed, so that no writer could possibly have further degraded her. And it was probably the success of this play that caused Henslowe to order another, on a similar theme, from Dekker and Chettle. On April 7, 1599, he loaned them three pounds " in earneste of ther boocke called Troyeles & creasse daye," [79] and on April 16 twenty shillings " in pte of payment of ther boocke called Troyelles & cresseda." [80] The play is not extant, but among the Henslowe papers there is a rough plot of a Troilus-Cressida play which may have been this one. A section of it runs thus:

> Enter Cressida wth Beggars, pigg Stephen, mr Jones his boy
> & mutes to them Troylus, & Deiphobus & proctor exeunt,[81]—

wrote that they had been " often (and not with the least applause,) Publickely Acted by two Companies, vppon one Stage at once." This performance may have been given during the autumn of 1597, when from October 11 to November 5 Pembroke's and the Admiral's men played together at the Rose. Fleay (*Biographical Chronicle*, vol. I, p. 285) believed this, but Greg (*Diary*, vol. II, p. 180) denies it. Nevertheless, among the inventory of properties owned by the Admiral's men (Heywood's company) on March 10, 1597/8, there was a " great horse with his leages " (*Henslowe Papers*, ed. Greg, p. 118), a property absolutely necessary for the second part of the *Iron Age* and very probably used for it during the performances of the preceding winter. Heywood's *Golden Age, Silver Age,* and *Brazen Age* seem to have been first performed on March 5, 1594/5, May 7, 1595, and May 23, 1595 (*Dairy*, ed. Greg, vol. II, p. 175; Fleay, *Biog. Chron.,* vol. I, pp. 283-284, and *History of the Stage,* p. 114); and it seems highly probable that the *Iron Age* immediately followed these. The best discussion of the date of the *Iron Age* is that in Professor Tatlock's " Siege of Troy," *PMLA.*, vol. XXX, pp. 707-719. He decides (p. 719) that " an earlier date for *Iron Age* than for Shakespeare's *Troilus* (1601-02) is favored by some of [the] evidence and opposed by none of it."

[79] Henslowe's *Diary*, ed. Greg, vol. I, 104.

[80] *Ibid.* The play of *Agamemnon* which was entered on May 26 and May 30, 1599 (*ibid.*, p. 109), Greg (*ibid.*, vol. II, p. 202) does not believe to have been the same as the Dekker-Chettle *Troilus.*

[81] *Henslowe Papers*, ed. Greg, p. 142.

enough to show that Henryson's poem had decidedly colored the plot.

Heywood probably got most of his material from Lydgate, though he also knew the *Iliad* and from it took his Thersites. But he has a number of remarkable deviations from Lydgate's narrative, many of them due, no doubt, to his knowledge of Homer. He seems not to have known Chaucer's *Troilus*,[82] but the final scene in which his Cressid appears is taken from Henryson's poem. "Pandors" is once used as a common noun,[83] but Pandarus is nowhere mentioned; and while Troilus is exalted to a position almost equal to that of Hector (as in Chaucer and Lydgate), the chronology of the love story is hopelessly muddled, and the characterization of Cressid is absurd. The outline of the story will indicate many points of resemblance between the *Iron Age* and Shakespeare's play.[84]

Troilus appears in the first scene of Act I, Part I, where

[82] But in his *Troia Britanica*, 1609 (note to Canto XI, p. 254), Heywood refers to the story of Troilus and Cressida written by "the reuerent Poet Chaucer."

[83] Pt. II, Act v (*Plays*, ed. Pearson, vol. III, p. 428).

[84] It is altogether improbable that, as almost all critics have said, Shakespeare took his Thersites directly from Chapman's *Iliad*. Instead he must have been chiefly influenced by Heywood's play, or by an older play which they both used. Perhaps he knew John Heywood's (?) interlude of *Thersites*, which was printed by Tyndale, 1552-1563; and certainly the scenes in which this Thersites abuses his old mother are as disgusting from the modern point of view and as amusing from the Elizabethan point of view as anything said by Shakespeare's Thersites. Shakespeare also knew Thersites from Arthur Golding's translation of the *Metamorphoses* (1567). The epigram on Thersites in Bastard's *Chrestoleros* (Spenser Society reprint, p. 28), which was published in April, 1598, some time before Chapman's *Iliad* first appeared, probably was suggested by the popularity of the Thersites in Heywood's *Iron Age*. Shakespeare's Thersites, like his Pandar, was intended to be purely a comic figure. See Heywood's comments on Thersites in his *Pleasant Dialogues and Dramas*, 1637 (no pagination or signatures).

Antenor is reporting his ill success at securing "Aunt Hesione" from the Greeks. Paris then secures permission to sail for Greece and steal Helen. The remainder of the act deals with his reception in Greece, the rape of Helen, and the arming of the Greeks for pursuit. Thersites appears in the first Grecian scene, "rayling" bitterly, calling Helen an "asse," predicting that Menelaus will soon wear horns, and otherwise disporting himself for the delectation of the groundlings. In Act II Troilus and Cressida are seen mutually pledging eternal faithfulness. Meanwhile Helen has been joyfully received into Troy, and the Greek hosts have encamped before the walls. Calchas then flees, Hector vows vengeance on him, but not a word is said of Cressid. After a skirmish or two, Hector steps between the ranks, offering to stake the outcome of the war on single combat. Ulysses suggests that the Greek champion be determined by lot. In the combat that follows, Hector refuses to fight to the bitter end because Ajax is his cousin. Priam then invites the Greek kings to a banquet.

Act III opens with the banquet. Hector graciously welcomes his cousin, calmly listens to Achilles's predictions of how and where he will be killed, and seems unaware that Calchas is present whispering to Cressid. Presently the father and daughter have this ridiculous conversation:

> *Cal.* In one word this *Troy* shall be sackt and spoil'd,
> For so the gods haue told mee, *Greece* shall conquer,
> And they be ruin'd, leaue then imminent perill,
> And flye to safety.
>
> *Cres.* From *Troilus?*
>
> *Cal.* From destruction, take *Diomed* and liue,
> Or *Troilus* and thy death.
>
> *Cres.* Then *Troilus* and my ruine.
>
> *Cal.* Is *Cresid* mad?
> Wilt thou forsake thy father, who for thee
> And for thy safety hath forsooke his Countrey?

Cres. Must then this City perish?
Cal. *Troy* must fall.
Cres. Alas for *Troy* and *Troilus.*
Cal. Loue King *Diomed*
　　　A Prince and valiant, which made Emphasis
　　　To his Imperiall stile, liue *Diomeds* Queene,
　　　Be briefe, say quickly wilt thou? is it done?
Cres. *Diomed* and you i'le follow, *Troilus* shun.

She has hardly ceased speaking when a quarrel begins between Diomed and Troilus, from which we learn that Diomed has already captured Troilus's horse and sent it as a gift to Cressid. The banquet breaks up in confusion. Nothing is told of Cressid's departure or of the grief of Troilus, but soon after, in a brief scene, Troilus fights Diomedes, knocks off his helmet, and when the Greek has fled, apostrophizes his sweetheart as " false Cresida," and irrationally closes the scene by exclaiming:

My Steede hee got by sleight, I this [the helmet] by force.
I'le send her this to whom hee sent my horse.

In Act IV Diomedes and Troilus enter " after an alarum " for a four-line scene, in which the Trojan declares, " I'le live to loue [Cressid] when thy life is past." Achilles now treacherously surrounds Hector with his Myrmidons, kills him, and drags the corpse at the tail of his horse, thus upsetting all mediæval legend and no doubt preparing for the similar incident in Shakespeare's play. Troilus is likewise surrounded and killed by Achilles; but the villainous Greek is shortly afterward enticed to Troy and shot by Paris. Act V ends with the suicide of Ajax and an epilogue by Thersites.

In Part II Cressid fares badly, probably not so much because Heywood had any bitterness for her as because the thousand and one details he crowded into his play prevented his giving close attention to making her consistent and realistic. Heywood is notably poor in motivating women characters: the ease with which Mrs. Frankford, in his masterpiece, yields to Wendoll, is sufficient proof of this defect; but his presentation of Cressid is nothing short of ridiculous.

In the first act (among a dozen other scenes) Diomedes remarks to Sinon: " Goe with me to my Tent, this night we'le reuell With beauteous *Cressida.*" Sinon reproaches Diomed for loving her, and when Diomed says, " Shee is both constant, wise, and beautifull," replies in a speech that is decidedly reminiscent of Henryson:

> She's neither constant, wise, nor beautifull,
> Ile prooue it *Diomed:* foure Elements
> Meete in the structure of that *Cressida,*
> Of which there's not one pure: she's compact
> Meerely of blood, of bones and rotten flesh,
> Which makes her Leaprous.

When Diomedes protests, Sinon offers to prove his statement. Cressida approaches, Diomedes steps aside, and Sinon accosts her. I am going to meet Diomedes, she tells him, and lead him with kisses to his tent; he is a fair and comely personage, whom I love as my life. " Personage ? " says Sinon, " ha, ha. I prithee looke on me, and view me well, And thou wilt find some difference." She scorns him, but listens when he begs her to leave her lover and come with him. He tells her that Diomedes has a queen in Etolia who will kill her. For a moment she wavers. " Love me, Cressid," says Sinon; " come kiss me," and this amazing creature replies:

> Well, you may vse your pleasure;
> But good *Synon* keep this from *Diomed.*

The whole change takes place in fifty lines. Diomed then appears, justly banishes her from his sight, and leaves her lamenting her betrayal. Penthesilea enters, hears her grievance against Sinon, and promises to avenge her (a promise, however, that is not fulfilled), while Cressid presumably goes straight to Troy. A last glimpse of her comes when, the wooden horse having brought the Greeks into the city, she and Helen are running wildly to escape. Says Helen:

> Death, in what shape soeuer hee appeares
> To me is welcome, I'le no longer shun him;
> But here with *Cresida* abide him: here,
> Oh, why was *Hellen* at the first so faire,
> To become subiect to so foule an end?
> Or how hath *Cresids* beauty sinn'd 'gainst Heauen,
> That it is branded thus with leprosie?

Cressid answers:

> I in conceit thought that I might contend
> Against Heauens splendor, I did once suppose,
> There was no beauty but in *Cresids* lookes.

She does not mention Troilus or her own double falsity, and with this speech she passes from the play. Heywood seems to have brought her in here only because she was always written of and thought of as a leper: having thus satisfied the Elizabethan mania for " historical accuracy," he was content to let her pass, sure that his audience could finish out her story. And so he carries his lumbering play through two more acts until he has brought all the Greek kings, Helen, Thersites, and Sinon to their violent deaths.

The resemblances between the *Iron Age* and *Troilus and Cressida* are striking, and one must decide that Shakespeare was influenced by the earlier play or that both he and Heywood used a common source.

There is really no problem in regard to Shakespeare's attitude towards the three major characters of the love story. In the third act of *Troilus* [85] he makes Pandar say: " If ever you prove false to one another, since I have taken

[85] III, ii, 205 ff.

such pains to bring you together, let all pitiful goers-between be called to the world's end after my name; call them all Panders; let all constant men be Troiluses, all false women Cressids, and all brokers—between Pandars! say, Amen." All say " Amen " in a scene that must have been irresistibly comic, for Pandarus had simply stated a fact. At that very moment Troilus was the name for a constant lover, " Cressid's kind " was the ordinary euphemism for " harlot," " pander " had become a common noun. Shakespeare, then, had little choice in the matter; he was obliged to portray these three characters as time and tradition had fixed them.

Dr. Small was wrong in saying that Shakespeare " adopts the character of Pandarus from Chaucer without change,"[86] and Miss Porter equally wrong in maintaining that " Chaucer turned [Pandarus] into a trusty, true-hearted old uncle, and Shakespeare re-created [him] in a gay, gross, shrewd, and worldly courtier-type peculiarly his own, despite the nucleus of the older suggestion ";[87] for there is nothing whatever of the courtier-type, no individuality whatever, about Shakespeare's Pandarus. He is merely a type of the pimp that Elizabethans were accustomed to see prowling about the streets or in Paul's. Shakespeare saw in him a good part for a low comedian; he made Pandar a buffoon, the butt of the play, but did not try to raise him from common " noundom." That would have been a hope·less task; and Shakespeare adjusted his characterization to the noun, just as the writers of the Moralities had tried to present characters that would fit such names as Simplicity, Perseverance, or Fraud. " Pander " had become a generic name early in the century, and by Shakespeare's

[86] *The Stage-Quarrel*, p. 155.
[87] *Troilus and Cressida*, First Folio ed., p. 138.

day it was necessary to use some qualifying word or phrase
when the individual Pandarus was meant. Thomas Lodge,
for instance, wrote in the preface to his *Wits Miserie*
(1596): " Earthly Deuils in humane habits, . . . wait on
your tasters when you drinke . . . and become Panders
if you hire them," and later: " Behold another more hain-
ous spirit . . . who . . . must to Poules presently to
meet with his *Pandare*." [88]   But when he wished to make
a distinct allusion to the legendary character Pandarus he
wrote: " [Cousenage] is the excellent of her age at a ring
& a basket: & for a baudie bargain, I dare turne her loose
to CHAUCERS *Pādare*." [89]   The noun " pander " is
used five times in *Eastward Ho* (1603), a play in which
Tamberlaine, Hieronimo, and Hamlet are burlesqued; and
it seems very probable that if Shakespeare's contemporaries
had seen any individuality in his characterization of the
go-between, Jonson and his collaborators would have burlesqued Shakespeare's Pandar instead of using his name
only as a class designation.

Even before he wrote *Troilus and Cressida* Shakespeare
had followed the fashion in regard to the three figures of
the love story. " Marry, sir," Ford tells Falstaff, " we'll
bring you to Windsor, to one Master Brook, that you have
cozen'd of money, to whom you should have been a pander." [90]   " Troilus," says Benedick, was " the first em-
ployer of panders "; [91] while Bourbon cries: " And he

[88] Lodge's *Works*, Hunterian Club ed., vol. IV, pp. 5-6, 57.

[89] *Ibid.*, p. 44. So in Beaumont and Fletcher's *Woman Hater*, 1607,
one of the characters is called Pandar (the common noun), and has
quite as much individuality as Shakespeare's Pandarus. " Sir Pandarus, be my speed! " they make him exclaim when the proper noun
is meant. Cf. the poetical description of " A Pander " in Rowlands's
Knave of Clubs, 1609, sign. A4 (Hunterian Club ed., vol. II, p. 7).

[90] *Merry Wives*, v, v, 176.

[91] *Much Ado*, v, ii, 31.

that will not follow Bourbon now, Let him go hence, and with his cap in hand, Like a base pandar, hold the chamber door." [92] But when Chaucer's Pandarus is meant, a specific reference is necessary. Says Pistol, " Shall I Sir Pandarus of Troy become, And by my side wear steel ? " [93] " I am Cressid's uncle," Lafeu remarks as he presents Helena to the King, " That dare leave two together; fare you well." [94]

Rosalind names Troilus as " one of the patterns of love," [95] Petruchio calls his puppy Troilus,[96] and Lorenzo, reminiscent of Chaucer, tells Jessica,

> In such a night as this . . .
> Troilus methinks mounted the Troyan walls,
> And sigh'd his soul toward the Grecian tents,
> Where Cressid lay that night.[97]

But poor Cressida fared worse. " Would not a pair of these have bred, sir ? " asks the Clown when Viola has given him a piece of money. " I would play Lord Pandarus of Phrygia, sir, to bring a Cressida to this Troilus." Viola answers, " I understand you, sir. 'Tis well begg'd "; and in his reply the Clown goes straight back to Henryson: " The matter, I hope, is not great, sir, begging but a beggar. Cressida was a beggar." [98] These words must have had much point, for the audiences that were seeing *Twelfth Night* had only a short time before seen the *Iron Age,* in which Cressida is smitten with leprosy, and the Dekker-Chettle *Troilus,* in which she comes on the stage with a swarm of beggars. It would have been nothing short of marvelous if Shakespeare had had any other conception of

---

[92] *Henry V,* IV, v, 14.
[93] *Merry Wives,* I, iii, 83.
[94] *All's Well,* II, i, 100.
[95] *As You Like It,* IV, i, 97.
[96] *Taming of the Shrew,* IV, i, 153.
[97] *Merchant of Venice,* V, i, 6.
[98] *Twelfth Night,* III, i, 55 ff.

her. And it is Pistol who degrades the poor woman to the depths where Whetstone, Howell, and Willobie had already shoved her. Jealous of the attentions Nym is paying to Mrs. Pistol, the irate husband cries out:

> O hound of Crete, think'st thou my spouse to get?
> No! to the spittal go,
> And from the powdering-tub of infamy,
> Fetch forth the lazar kite of Cressid's kind,
> Doll Tearsheet she by name.[99]

No such conception of Cressid appears in *Troilus and Cressida*. Did Shakespeare intentionally avoid it?

It is almost certain that Shakespeare thought the *Testament* to be Chaucer's own work. In the play, no doubt through the medium of Speght's 1598 edition, he borrows liberally from Chaucer's poem, and I think it highly probable that Alexander's remark about Ajax (I, ii, 15)—" He is a very man *per se,* And stands alone "—was suggested by a phrase Shakespeare found in the " sixth book " of the *Troilus*—" O fayre Cresside the flour and *A per se* of Troy and Grece "—and that originally he wrote, " He is a very *A per se.*" [100] Cressida's petulant remark to Dio-

---

[99] *Henry V*, II, i, 76.

[100] In 1748 John Upton, in his *Observations on Shakespeare* (Miss Spurgeon, vol. I, p. 397), wrote: " Plausible as this reading [" he is a very man *per se* "] appears, it seems to me originally to come from the corrector of the press. For our poet I imagine made use of Chaucer's expression [*i. e.*, Henryson's " *A per se* "], from whom he borrowed so many circumstances in the play." Upton was right, I think; and if *he* confused Chaucer and Henryson in 1748, surely it was not surprising for Shakespeare to do this in 1600 and to borrow, perhaps unconsciously, the phrase which he had read in Chaucer's works.

According to the *New English Dictionary*, Henryson first used the phrase. It came early to be a commonplace among the Scotch poets— see, for example, Sibbald's *Chronicle of Scottish Poetry*, vol. III, pp. 169, 187, 361, 363, 495; *Gude and Godlie Ballatis*, ed. A. F. Mitchell, p. 147—but was not especially common in England before 1600. In

medes (V, ii, 89 f.), " 'Twas one's that lov'd me better than you will," is unquestionably a reference to Henryson's story; and when she finally surrendered to Diomedes, crying, " Ay, come—O Jove!—do come. I shall be *plagu'd* " (V, ii, 105), her hearers must surely have thought of the *Testament*. But one can only marvel—as Dryden, who knew almost nothing of the history of the story, did for other reasons—at the ending of the play which leaves both Troilus and Cressida alive.

Dr. Georg Brandes found in Shakespeare's attitude towards Cressida " passionate heat and hatred," " boundless bitterness." " His mood is the more remarkable in that he in no wise paints her as unlovable or corrupt; she is merely a shallow, frivolous, sensual, pleasure-loving coquette . . . Shakespeare has aggravated and pointed every circumstance until Cressida becomes odious, and rouses only aversion. One is astounded by the bitterness of the hatred he discloses." [101] In the light of the history of the love story, the remarkable thing really is that Shakespeare dealt with her so mildly, for the subject of the play must have been extremely distasteful to him. Certainly he has no apparent bitterness towards Cressida: he does not punish her as did Henryson; he does not make her a common harlot as did Henryson, Whetstone, Howell, and the rest; nor does he make her the wholly contemptible creature of

Turbervile's *Tragical Tales*, 1587 (Edinburgh reprint, 1837, p. 297), occur the lines:

> That famous Dame, fayre Helen, lost her hewe
> When withred age with wrinckles chaungd her cheeks,
> Her louely lookes did loathsomnesse ensewe,
> That was the A per se of all the Greekes.

The fact that Turbervile was so fond of referring to the Henryson story, as well as the context of the above lines, makes it practically certain that *he* borrowed the phrase from Henryson.

[101] *William Shakespeare* (English translation), London, 1898, pp. 193-194.

Heywood's or the miserable leprosy-stricken beggar of the Dekker-Chettle play.

When one considers also the other arguments that have been advanced by critics, it seems probable that in 1599 Shakespeare's play was ordered by the Chamberlain's company to compete with the two Troy plays of the Admiral's men, that for some reason it was not finished and " clapperclawed with the palms of the vulgar " but was put aside for a year or two, and that the last few scenes, the work of another hand with slight revisions by Shakespeare, were, added for the performance about 1602. For it is almost incredible that, with his knowledge of Henryson, his preconceived ideas of the character of Cressid and the reward of her treachery, and his respect for what the public wanted, Shakespeare should have ended his play without at least punishing Cressid. How can the present ending have pleased his audiences? Even the groundlings, how-ever much delighted with Thersites and Pandar, surely were dissatisfied when the play abruptly dropped the leading characters instead of carrying them on to the logical and traditional *dénouement*. What American audience would care to see *Uncle Tom's Cabin* if no Little Eva appeared in the cast or if Eliza failed to cross the ice? Shakespeare, if he wrote all the play, wrenched the familiar story as violently in one direction as Dryden later did in another; neither version could have been satisfactory in 1602.

Apart from the absurd mercenary puff in the preface to the quarto of 1609, this " Commedie " received no contemporary praise. When Mr. John Munroe published the *Shakspere Allusion-Book* in 1909, he could point out only three references to *Troilus and Cressida* before 1650; two of these—Dekker's mention in *The Wonderful Year* (1604) of " false Cressida," which is purely conventional but as much an allusion to his own play as to Shakespeare's, and a line in Marston's *Dutch Courtesan* (1605), " Sometimes a fall out proves a falling in," which is said to be an imitation of Pandar's " Falling in after falling out may make them three "—do not seem to me to be allusions to Shakespeare. Of the sixteen allusions given for the years 1650-1700, one is a remark in Collier's *Short View* that " Shakespear makes Hector quote Aristotle's philosophy," another Dryden's discussion of the play in the preface to his revision of it, six are quotations inserted in Cotgrave's *English Treasury* (1655), and the other eight are matter-of-fact statements in Langbaine's work on the dramatic poets. Shakespeare had no influence whatever on the Troilus-Cressida story. He himself never again referred to Troilus or Cressida or Pandar; and although their story was not so popular in the seventeenth as in the sixteenth century, yet there are bountiful allusions up to 1640 to the constancy of Troilus, the falsity and leprosy of Cressid.

When in 1679 Dryden resurrected the play, refurbished it, and invented Cressida's constancy, he found himself chiefly pleased by the characters Pandar and Thersites. Furthermore, although he declared that " the original story was written by one Lollius, a Lombard, in Latin verse, [and was] intended, I suppose, a satire on the inconstancy of women," he saw no bitterness or satire, no jealousy, no debasement of the classical heroes, but only early experimentation, in Shakespeare's *Troilus and Cressida*. As that play stands, indeed, Cressida has been decidedly pulled out of the mire in which Henryson's followers had placed her. Yet we could feel surer that Shakespeare was responsible for all of the play if he had punished Cressida,—if in portraying her he had unmistakably shown bitterness and hatred.

HYDER E. ROLLINS.